The Breath before Birds Fly

Poems By
M. E. Silverman

Copyright © 2013 M. E. Silverman
Copyright © 2013 Cover Art "Rose-breasted Grosbeak" by Mary Sneddon
2nd Place - 2013 ELJ Publications Chapbook Competition

All rights reserved.
ISBN: 978-0615783055

While this book is indebted to all the love and support I receive from family, friends, colleagues and editors, this book is ultimately dedicated to you, the reader.

Toda Raba (הבר הדות) *Thanks Much*

CONTENTS

Fumes	3
Mud Angel	4
After You Left	5
Water Dreams: Hurricane Katrina	6
Noah Shops for an Ark	8
Rain Chaser	10
When the Barn Door Shuts	12
What I Know about Jerusalem Rain	13
Bubbie's Kitchen Secret	15
Echo Locating	17
Why I Don't Talk to my Brother	18
The Freak from Kulakousky Street	20
Angelito del Fango	22
Mud Man	23
The Talker	25
Ritual for Learning History	26
After	27
The Last Mermaid	28
Miracle Shoes	30
At the Altar of Water	32
Slipping	33
The Last Jew	34
The Last Jew (ii)	38

ACKNOWLEDGMENTS

Several poems in this collection have been published in the following journals and anthologies (some in slightly different forms): *BatterSea Review*, *Blood Orange Review*, *Chicago Quarterly Review*, *Cooweescoowee*, *Crab Orchard Review*, *Front Range Review*, *Generations*, *Hawai'i Pacific Review*, *Neon*, *New Vilna Review*, *Pembroke Magazine*, *The Southern Poets Anthology, Volume V: Georgia*, *Story South*, and *Vision/Verse*. Grateful acknowledgment is made to the hard-working editors and staff of these publications.

Fumes

The day mother and I leave, two
Canada geese arrive—
their long, black necks arrow
toward the pond and fold into themselves
like cocktail napkins. I hoped
they'd stay there forever.
The afternoon burnishes
Mother from freckle-red to bruised-peach,
a glass of brewed tea
left out and discolored.
Ladybugs cling to the apple-red
of the front door, a small
mosquito meals on my arm,
and a solitary squirrel digs for nuts.

After a day of packing, she rushes
me into the car, exhaust fumes sputter
moons. This is June:
dust blots the glass,
love bugs and moths
smear the customized grill.
The car trembles with purpose.
In the back seat, I
wait. An orange bear
pillows my bruised head.
On the busted porch,
Father crushes cans, smokes
Strikes. Mother peals away—
runs over the white mailbox.

Mud Angel

In the barn, he removes
and folds his clipped wings,

a blue-gray from age,
not from dye but grime and storage.

Gently, the long feathers
brush the scar on his left cheek.

At night, in flight,
it itches more

like a healing wound
open to air. Every morning,

every morning he looks down
from the loft, rests

a hand on one bale of hay,
thinks about chores and closes

the trunk, thick with dust and dirt,
then turns, his back bare with ghost limbs.

Earth. Nothing more.
Let that be enough.

After You Left

After a night of summer storms
and the jagged, in-drawn breath
of funnels that seized century old roots
from the earth
and tossed two oaks
onto my lot,
I roam my land with caution
to repair what I can.

I arrive on this plank-board bridge
built before you left.

I push aside a path
through a net of twigs, kneel

on tender knees, I cup my hands
to drink from the downpours'
settled waters,
risen high.

A mockingbird squawks nearby,
light and full of air,

owning nothing.
We each eye the other

between the maple's flames
and a bank of daffodils,

limp
from the weight of rain.

Water Dreams: Hurricane Katrina

Because I always wanted one,
my father has pulled a hairless cat
out of my chest.
He tells me about Abraham in Hebrew
the way his father taught him.
I stare at the door in his lips.
My ears are full of winter.
I try to hear, I really do.
Water presses against my body,
pushes salty grime inside my mouth, my nose, every pore.
It swallows the sun.
Darkness soaks through me,
makes me heavy and sleepy.
He lifts me from the water,
whispers words from the only stories he knows,
says God calls Abraham to the land,
gives them a child late in life, calls them chosen.

A part of me knows my father is not God
and cannot breathe life into something so small as me,
curled like the crescent moon this city is named after.
I want to tell him something important
as I hear him slap and slap the animal,
first soft like a clap during service's joy,
then hard like a stomp during service's dances
until a loud smack like when I've been bad.

Above me, mumbling close to my face, his voice is scratchy
like when he sings to Muddy Waters and Louis. Everything looks
foggy, sounds like gargling. He says Noah would never have saved
a sinner like me. I should stop my crying, start swimming so the great

river can see me and keep me from going under, down where
our house and car are taken back by the Almighty.

Then I hear a trumpet warming up.
A hungry noise,
a gator's open-teeth snap.

I breathe and breathe
and obey for the love of God,
the way Isaac did with his eyes closed,
without murmuring, aware of the sharp steel
but not what his father hears,
what his father knows,
yet still willing to go
through the floating door.

Noah Shops for an Ark

After God asks,
Noah, not bothering to dress,

goes to Lowes.
He wanders aisles,

past tubes and buckets, pails and bulbs,
stacks of pipes, sheets of colorful metal.

He spots a clerk steadily sweeping twigs,
looking more bored than busy.

The clerk chooses to ignore the old robe,
open, exposing a nest of hairs.

The entire stock of nails?
ponders the clerk straining against sleep.

And boards. Gopher wood. All sizes.
Ready to repeat the request,

Noah, nervous and sweaty,
crumples onto a small stack

of hollow display boxes.
Oh God! Sir,

are you okay?
Sir, are you

okay?
Sir?

In the morning,
Noah pours us both tea.

Over runny eggs
and lightly burnt toast,

he recalls the reoccurring dream
while I eat and nod,

staring into eyes wild
with birds.

Rain Chaser

Forget that *all water has a perfect memory*
and is forever trying to get back
to where it was.

Give me this moment
without his violent storms
in a motel where I now sleep alone.

Let me listen to distant moans
and lovely laughter, to the way weather
moves, how raindrops slant,

sound like marbles spilling on a floor,
seeping into every dry spot,
remembering where it used to be.

A westerly gale swirls
and in the harbor, nervous boats bounce.
The river floods these places.

Signs and tree limbs knock about
against spaces they don't want to go.
The wind shoves them down.

I know these forces,
these shifting skies.
I'm drawn to thunder.

I pick up the phone.
Dial our number.
Rain descends

on this soaked roof,
runs down spouts and windows,
upon sills and the backs of bricks,

fills a barricaded pool, pushes
beneath this foundation
where a water particle is more likely to go

to where it has gone before,
where water dreams in cyanotype
and everything drowns out of focus.

When the Barn Door Shuts

> *"We have all forgotten an incredible secret."*
> ~ Eugene Ionesco

Father sees trees split by frost,
mud, work not done,
and sometimes, a salvation

in the lamplight beneath the porch,
removing overalls and shoes
covered with the day's dirt and sweat streaks,

darker than his hair, darker than failure,
where he hesitates before going in
to meatloaf or stew in her barren kitchen,

as soil drips down his face,
tastes like love,
salt and iron,

and the song he hears
resides in winds, in seed counts,
in the crouch and pull and lift,

measuring distance between two
fields. Listen: it sounds like roots
ripped up, like metal turning

through soil. Soon, he forgets the lexicon
for the way earth cakes to skin,
how each season stretches to say:

stay,
tomorrow,
good.

What I Know about Jerusalem Rain

In the oldest part of a city
ghosting with holiness,
I couldn't stop thinking about how half
of our bodies are simply water
even though most of our days
are dry rote, except here,
coming through ceiling cracks
and the small space
around our window's
seals, is this rain
that seeps into the deep
of seas and beds
like tears, carves a path
through earth, through the hurt
of shards
and all the layers
of foundation
buried beneath our feet,
the hidden support
for our small steps,
and how when it storms,
when it really storms,
wind shatters windows,
pushes through plaster
and washes over everything
we made.

Maybe then we take what we can,
head toward something solid,
toward the ark we imagine we built
when we were young,
still stock-piling

for a future for two.
Maybe then with breath
big enough for a Shofar,
we will begin to wade
through these waters.
.

Bubbie's Kitchen Secret

Hell's Kitchen, New York City 1983

We cooked in her kitchen,
a small square room
with a large double sink.
The refrigerator zapped
its electric ache
and like an old noir film,
the lights flickered in response.

For herbs, she had me climb
onto the counter and open
the one window to reach
the basil, the thyme, the sunflowers
potted on the fire escape,
a hazardous garden
the whole building used.

Two or three steps were lined
with mason jars full of cucumbers,
for pickles crisp from sunlight.

On this particular Sabbath,
I did what I always did,
helped her make the kugel,
a pudding made of noodles and eggs
with a dash of her secret:
the caramel color from sugar burnt:
not too little, not too much.

We were finishing up
when we smelled the cigar smoke

and heard heavy boots
pounding down the fire escape.

Then glass breaking,
a curse, *that* curse,
quick and sharp
in gun-shot German.

Bubbie screamed. Scared,
I ducked under the table.
She whispered one word
before fainting.
My gold-chained *chai*
fell fast, a train bell's echo.

Echo Locating

If you are lucky
you will find your echo,
not the cartoon version,
perched on a canyon's edge
with the empty yelling
and cheeks like apples,
but the space that extends you,
fills the void
and becomes you
the way twigs return to a tree,
nest-warm.

Why I Don't Talk to My Brother
For Phil

The bittersweet tea scent of after rain
seeps into my skin.

A honeysuckled wind hints early winter,
lingers in everything.

The swift hush of trucks rushes by.
Squirrels scavenge outside my family room.

A few blue jays and two finches
swoop from their perch to scoop seeds from my feeder.

Since I am busy writing, my yard goes untended;
the ground drowns in oak and pine.

I notice the next-door neighbors
through my savage tree barrier.

Packed on their back porch,
they drink beer and point guns at unseen deer.

Two older men in overalls
play dominoes, bite whole apples.

One cups his hand on his chin,
a pink gummed smile when he slaps tiles.

They seem so close with each other
even the teen who waves his free hand

like a conductor, raising his voice above the others.
So much noise—I almost call the sheriff,

but I know this is more about losing
their war hero brother.

A small part of me wants to pretend I know their grief,
try to guzzle away emotion

and not carry my anger
like an oversized parcel.

It should be that simple.
But I am caught with my own work.

For a time, I see
how they fill a space,

I place their hunger with my own,
while I listen to the hollow hum,

undialed. I replace the receiver
and write a first line:

The bittersweet tea scent of after rain.

The Freak from Kulakousky Street

> *"There on trails past knowing / Are tracks of beast you never met;*
> *On chicken feet a hut is set / With neither door nor window showing...*
> *See Baba-Yaga's mortar glide / All of itself, with her astride."*
> ~ Pushkin's "Ruslan and Ludmila" trans. Jenni Blackwood

She wakes in Yakutsk.
Trees are silent
with frost,
bitter like iron chains.

She haunts houses
and bridges,
trucks stuck until spring,
caught in winter's secret layers.

Suspended crystals
create rainbows.
Fog freezes in Lenin Square.
Commuters continue onward.

White hurts the horizon.
Only the students stop
with change.
She wonders what they know of this.

When others notice her, the hag,
it is in the unsaid, brittle looks
like muddy fences
ready to bend and break,
in throats filled with the brunt
of biting days,
and in their persistent stares
that rattles through anything warm.

People pass her by.
She shouts, "I am
not Baba Yaga!
My cabin is not on chicken feet!"

Sometimes she coughs,
cold and agitated,
waves small bones
to the wind.

Children run by, poke
her big behind
with twigs. They chant
"here comes the witch!"

Rumor has it:
she eats children, cats too,
says her silver birch broom
hides in her heart.

They will never know how
to face the world,
stand savage with all one has,
how winter deforms

like a distorted whistle,
a train in the ears.

They will never know how
her longing lasts.

Angelito del Fango

> *In November 1966, the Arno River in Florence overflowed, killing 33 and displacing 5000 families. In addition, 600,000 tons of debris and mud damaged 15,000 cars, 14,000 pieces of art and 3 million books. The people from Florence called those that helped 'Angelito del Fango' or Mud Angels.*

When my father first heard about the flood, he boarded a train
from France. He did not go for the people or the city; he hoped
to save Italy's artistic legacy by removing works of art
from their mud-filled cells. He did not expect brown splotches
on rooftops, overturned cars, uprooted trees and packed layers
smudged on homes, on churches and bubbles on every street
like German measles. He almost turned back.

He did not speak the language, but lugged Italian books that smelled
like sour underlog from the Biblioteca Nazionale Centrale Firenze
to Michelangelo's Fortress, five at a time, always five
for the purposes of counting. Sludge swarmed up his clothes,
through his skin, down his throat. All day, sun and breeze, breeze
and sun. Still, he sang songs and prayed, foreign words rang
with the clapper of his tongue.

Near the end of his stay, he began to help clean the books
between a Russian and a Spaniard, dipping their brushes into resin
then ironing over the substance to turn it to powder. A slow process
to keep the ink on the pages.

Alone, at the train station,
windows, white floating tea lights,
filled his departure.

Mud Man

"Speak to the earth, and it shall teach you."
~ Job 12: 7-8

Needing a father, I create a *dybbuk*
of mire and soil and clay,
layered with discarded leaves
from a maple or live oak
with leaves green on one side,
packed from the seasoned bones
of extinct animals
and the rocks my daughter collects.

Together we chant our silly song:
Mud, mud, glorious mud
Nothing quite like it for cooling the blood
So follow me follow, down to the hollow
And there let me wallow in glorious mud.

When I call his name,
he bubbles to the top
like chemicals in a beaker.
When he sees me
with my daughter,
he scoops her onto shoulders
cloudy as smoke-oil,
takes us to Italian fields
filled with lavender and sunflower.

My mud man gives her all
the secrets the earth bares.
He responds to her sounds,
speaks about puddles,
how to walk without breaking twigs,

shaping dolls from reeds.
He nods with assiduous attention,
shows her where earthworms
are born, how termites travel
for food, the aureate gifts of the sun,
the wonder at a pond's bottom,
the fathomable kingdom of frogs.

The Talker

The last guest who goes on and on
is gone. Hearing the same stories again
is like listening to long poems
in a foreign language. Our ears ring,
as our guest talks like a drill sergeant
who never pauses, megaphone loud.

Now that he's gone, we move
about without speaking, picking up
this, adjusting that. Then we head
outside to sit on porch rockers,
hot tea in hands,
surrounded by lilac
and the spicy scent of gardenias.
We watch the occasional car
freely speed by
deep into the dull night.

Our minds center on bed
and the blanket's comfort—
the affectionate rhythm
of that other known body,
while the soapy, silent moon
gives what slender, tired light
it can.

Ritual for Learning a History

Father loves matzah balls more than me,
more than anyone. He doesn't pause for them
to cool, a child with his prize.

I wait for the four glasses of wine,
the bitter herbs, the tightening
of his eyes and cheeks,

his shoulders and arms,
as he tells the same stories
every year: how he sacrificed

so much to be a Dad
after his own deserted them
with the rabbi's most buxom daughter,

how he spent his monthly ten-cent treat
on sci-fi books, the buses it took to get
out of Sheepshead Bay,

how his mother threw away issue one
of Action, now worth a quarter of a million,
because he once asked where his Dad had gone,

how he shouted out the open door
about her refusal to learn to drive,
to move from the tired bricks of Brooklyn,

to breach her routine that lasted for forty years,
the hot months he peddled down Fifth like a commandment
and up First delivering silk for tips.

After

In the morning, after facts slip out like a tip,
we are not the same. Nothing more
to say

so I go like a deer run too far,
too fast, and you,
you are the hungry road,
the dense egg smell of roadside sulphur,
the pungent mark of burnt rubber.

I want to bolt back
to the over-grown field,
where birds quiz off key.

The Last Mermaid

On the quayside, she removes
and folds her clipped tail,

a gunk-gray from storage
and dust, not from age.

Scales soft as kelp
shimmer and brush

against the hook-shaped scar
on her right hip.

Monthly, she goes out,
slow, savors the flow

of the moonlit sea.
Mid-swim, it itches

like a bone healing.
Come morning,

when the shadow light fades
and the ocean changes color,

blends back to stale sky,
her hands hesitate

on the decaying dock,
her back to the rising sun,

thinks about house chores
and appointments to keep,

then lifts herself up
onto those limbs,

now awkward and exposed
like a crutch.

Miracle Shoes
- *United States Holocaust Memorial Museum*

One day, the stacked shoes begin to rise
leisurely, like puppets on strings.
At first people pour into the museum
to view the shoes floating about.
Like a curtain drawn back,
a chamber unlocked,
the shoes silently sweep through the air
like Astaire and Rogers.
The watchers whisper and point, gasp
and stare. The murmurs ache
with melody, violins in a symphony.
A girl in a green dress
thinks the shoes are waltzing
and the newspapers take to it,
begin referring to them
as Little Dancers—
laces like wired shadows.

Soon the other exhibits go unnoticed.
A few people gather outside
with candles and army-surplus blankets,
singing songs about being saved
and chanting prayers in unison.
This goes on for many nights
and everyone who hears them
is filled with a solemn beauty.
Some weep and others make silent vows.

Early on a Saturday in September,
an old security guard, coffee cup in hand
and *The Post* tucked under his arm,

holds the heavy doors open
a little too long,
and the shoes start to slip through,
swirling couples hover, the breath
before birds fly.

Later, he will be quoted
as saying he never did spill
a drop of coffee
or ruin his paper
but never did he think
about closing that door.

At the Altar of Water
Louisiana, 1996

Some evenings I almost think Elijah
walks in this swamp where I fish,
and have come to fish for forty years
between the towering trunks of Bald Cypress,
beneath the veils of Spanish moss.

I try to see from the corner of my eye
a holiness glide across these gray waters
that feel smaller with every year,
where waist-high Water Hyacinth
are invaders and paths are carved
through them like a scar,

so boats may pass like celebrities
amongst the paparazzi of weeds and wind,
while the cries of birds, ready to feed
but with no place to go, slowly starve.

I swat a mosquito with the palm of my hand,
flick away a broken wing,
ignore the golden heat on the back of my neck,
my arms, my legs, all the parts that ache.
I tie a knot to this line
and think slip, yes, let me slip
from my body like flying fish leap
to lose themselves
from the water's slow erasure.

Slipping

Minnows school and shift, pulse and pound, burst into sixty
or seventy slivers. Your hand in my hand, you take each step
as if walking in oversized slippers. Out here, crappies and perch
are abundant. Great gray owls and black-billed magpies fly by.
We stand by the water's edge. It doesn't know you're there,
that your legs, once so suited for this land, for swimming,
are now egret-thin. Now and then we pause. Rest is rote.
Dragonflies, like buzzing syringes, wing through the summer air.
Wasps and bees needle the breeze. It is too humid and late.
When we stop again, you remove your wig for the last time.
I rub your thin belly, circular and slow, to ease the ache.
Your shadow shimmers the water. I remember when we
were here last—your long Jewish curls flung droplets. You sung
Diamonds on the Soles of her Shoes" and told me histories that never
happened. When we return to the copse, we veer back toward
the path to sit some more. Near standing weeds, I think of Homer's
fields of asphodels. You stand and grit your teeth, hiss from
the effort and pluck a cluster of oval leaves. You toss the foliage
down, down to the moss-covered rock, shaped like oversized pills.
A yellow-bellied flycatcher swoops past. My narrow eyes stare
as it goes. I wonder about playing pool and jazz clubs, if I will take
a cruise or return to school somewhere abroad, and how fast life
will move when all this slowness ends.

The Last Jew

for Zablon Simintov, the last Jew of Afghanistan

I.   **Aliyah**

Sometimes we all feel like the last,
a single stick in a rushing river.
Honestly, who has not felt
hairs rise on the base of their neck
when hands cup to other ears
full of distressing whispers? Listen:

today you are the Last Jew.

You could be in Calcutta or Krakow,
any place given to time
for those *olim* who made *aliyah*.
"Next year in Jerusalem"
they said dutifully
until they did.

Today you are the Last

Jew, the chosen carpet dealer
in the heart of Kabul
where Hebrew letters breathe
like morning birds,
where echoes sink in surrounding streets,
unswept rooms and broken glass,
an eerie emptiness,
a staleness under cracked fans
and dusty cupboards
of books, hundreds
of years old, where God

grumbles to you and you alone.

Every Friday night,
the missing make a slight noise
that sounds like leaves,
sounds like sand,
like wings passing
by, flutters in the sky.

Do you hoist the Torah
above your shoulders, bear it
around the sanctuary for ghosts
to touch it with their *tallises*?
On the Sabbath, do you kiss
the book? Recite the prayers?
Who do you preach to? Who
in your synagogue is teaching?

"I don't know why I'm still
living here." To anyone
who cares, you say
the reason you stay, avoid
seeing your wife for over a decade
and your two Zionist children
is "God's will," but when
Moses confronted the pharaoh
or when Abraham left his home in Ur,
God never instructed them to become
like locust living off what the land offers,
to abandon their family.

So you watch, you wait—
we wonder. Today

you are the Last Jew.

II.   **Zablon's Reoccurring Dream**

In the Jerusalem Wing

the Tree of Life is empty.
This is no mistake.

Please believe.

We coated it with iron
stored it in a corner wing

the color of slate.

No cameras to record
the scene. Not even a guard.

Here in the Natural History Museum

in a section reserved
for the dioramas of the forgotten

one can take the tour

to see it
in the southwest corner.

For a fee.

III.   **Sabbath in the Last Temple**

Like a snoring old man,

the house of God
breathes still,
surprising the neighbors
as it inhales sand.

Nearby, vendors and traffic
sound like angry bees.
In the empty hour of the setting sun,
hounded by duty and tradition,
one Rabbi remains.

Like keys in a pocket
rattling and ready to go,
the holy house
shifts slow and steady, exhales
amber light, lush
as New Year honey.

The Last Jew (ii)

will be born sometime
> after
> you read this,

with matzah colored skin
> and Talmudic
> eyes,

> with the breath
> > of a lost language
> > that speaks
> > > to salt and ash,

> begins
> > with *baruch*,
> > beginning of a prayer,
> > > which most ignore

like the bearded veteran
> who holds a sign
> which could be a board
> > from the ark

on the corner
> of Main
> and 10th.
> > For a few,

> it will feel familiar
> > like the moment
> > right before

                a sneeze
                        and the bless
you, a fraction
of a second

where you know
                what will come next,
                and then

                it is
                gone.

NOTES

Many people have seen this manuscript at its various stages, but it owes much gratitude to the following people who helped shape the path: Deborah Ager, Karen Craigo, Kate Daniels (my first poetry instructor), Bernie Henrie, Meredith Kunsa, Jeffrey Levine, Fred Merchant, Ruth L. Schwartz, Judith Skillman, Elizabeth Klise von Zerneck, and John Wood (extra hugs). Also, I owe much thanks to all the folks at Colrain and Dzanc Creative Writing Sessions.

"Mud Angel" ends on two partial lines from Pedro Salinas: *Earth. Nothing more. / Earth. Nothing less. / Ana let that be enough for you.*

"Noah Shops for an Ark" is dedicated to Dr. John Wood who always wanted me to write a funny poem.

"When the Barn Door Shuts" and "Mud Angel" are both dedicated to everyone who helped me write this in McNeese's graduate program for creative writing.

"What I Know about Jerusalem Rain" is dedicated to Beatrice and our hurricane days.

"Why I Don't Talk to my Brother" is dedicated to my brother, Phil, in hopes he understands.

"The Freak from Kulakousky Street" is part of Slavic mythology where the old hag ("Baba Yaga") flies around in a mortar, using a broom to sweep away the tracks behind her. It is dedicated to Vika, the best Russian I know.

"Mud Man" is inspired by Mary Oliver's "Aunt Leaf". The lyrics are from "The Hippopotamus Song" by Flanders and Swann.

"The Talker" is dedicated to Karen.

"After" is inspired by William Matthews.

"Miracle Shoes" is inspired by all the imaginative tales Rita Silverman told me as a child.

"The Last Jew" is dedicated to Penny Schneier who passed away in 2012. In "I: Aliyah" there are lines used respectfully from Beckett's *Waiting for Godot*: "Vladimir: *They make a noise like wings.* / Estragon: *Like leaves.* / Vladimir: *Like sand.*"

GLOSSARY

Aliyah– the immigration to Israel, and it means "ascent".

Baba Yaga – folklore (Slavic), is an old witch who kidnaps children and lives in a hut that stands on chicken legs.

Baruch – bless (The first word of the prayers that always begin 'Bless the God' or "B*aruch atah Adonai*".).

Chai –means living and consists of the Hebrew alphabet *chet* and *yod*. It is a spiritual number in Judaism and symbol of life; many Jews give gifts of money in multiples of 18 as a result

Chuppah – is a canopy used for the wedding ceremony and is symbolic for home.

Dybbuk – folklore (Yiddish), and it means "attachment" because a malevolent spirit possesses the body of a living person.

Elijah – a prophet whose name is called upon during the Passover seder. It is interesting to note that in Romanian folklore Elijah the Thunderer is associated with summer storms.

Haggaddah –means "telling" and it is a text used for the order of Passover Seder that tells the story of what happened and allows Jews to remember being liberated from slavery in Egypt.

Matzah Balls– dumplings made from matzah meal and often served during Passover in soup. It is interesting to note that the largest ever made at Noah's Ark Deli weighed 267 pounds and was 29.2 inches long.

Olim– those who "make aliyah" are called an oleh (m. singular) or olah (f. singular) and the plural for both is olim.

Shalom – (Hebrew) meaning "peace, completeness, and welfare" but often used as a greeting and a parting as in hello and goodbye.

Shofar – a ram's horn used in religious services. It is blown in order to announce the new year in September called Rosh Hashanah, and again at Yom Kippur, ten days later.

Shul – a Jewish house of prayer, often called synagogue, meaning "assembly".

Tallises – a prayer shawl worn over the outer clothes during the morning prayers.

Talmud – one of the main Judaic texts, referring to Jewish laws, customs and history.

Yom Kippur – on the tenth day of the new year (which occurs in September), there is a holiday that is strictly for atonement.

ABOUT THE AUTHOR

M. E. Silverman, editor of the *Blue Lyra Review*, moved in the wake of Katrina from New Orleans to Georgia, where he now teaches at Gordon College. His work has appeared in 70 magazines including *Crab Orchard Review*, *Chicago Quarterly Review*, *Hawai'i Pacific Review*, *The Los Angeles Review*, *Pacific Review*, *Many Mountains Moving*, *Naugatuck River Review*, *The Broad River Review*, *Storysouth*, *The Southern Poetry Anthology*, *Sugar House Review*, *New Vilna Review*, *Cloudbank*, *Mizmor L'david Anthology: The Shoah*, *Because I Said So: Anthology*, *Knocking at the Door: Anthology*, and other journals and anthologies. M. E. Silverman was a finalist for the 2008 *New Letters* poetry award, the 2008 Denovo Contest and the 2009 *Naugatuck River Review* contest. Currently, he is working on editing a contemporary Jewish American anthology of poetry with Deborah Ager forthcoming from Bloomsbury Press (2013) and he is editing two other anthologies. He is also on the board of *32 poems*. He lives with his wife, his daughter, and Marie, the unwanted cat who daily breaks into their house through the heating vents.

Made in the USA
Charleston, SC
15 March 2013